C000121317

# THE FAMINE

By Harry Adès

Designed by Tony and Penny Mills

# the
# FAMINE

ᴄaᴙa

This edition published and distributed by Tara, 1999

Tara is an imprint of Parragon

Parragon
Queen Street House
4 Queen Street
Bath BA1 1HE

Produced by Magpie Books, an imprint of
Robinson Publishing Ltd, London

ISBN 1 90287 904 X

A copy of the British Library Cataloguing-in-Publication Data is available
from the British Library

Printed in China

## ACKNOWLEDGEMENTS

Colour plates on the cover and pp 2–3, 10–11, 28–9, 41, 44–5, 47, 54–5
and 57 are by the marine artist Rodney Charman, whose work is exhibited
here and in the USA. We are very grateful for his permission to reproduce
them here. They appear by courtesy of the Egan Foundation, Nantucket,
USA. Those on pp iii and 15 appear by courtesy of Mr Paul O'Hanlon.
Others are taken from articles that appeared in the
*Illustrated London News* and the *Graphic*.

# CONTENTS

Disaster Awaits                    4

Blight                             15

Famine                            21

Eviction                          32

Emigration                        40

The United States                 51

*(Above)* Evicted woman with all her possessions outside her house.
*(Overleaf)* The Perseverance, one of the first ships to carry emigrants
during the famine period directly from Dublin to New York, seen here
leaving Dublin on St Patrick's Day, 1846.

# Introduction

Two lifetimes ago, Ireland suffered perhaps the most terrible event of the nineteenth century. The potato famine of 1845–50 claimed the lives of over a million people, and drove millions of others from its shores. In just a couple of days in the summer of 1845, Ireland's fields were putrefying, the potatoes turning black as the stench of decay fouled the air. Most of the population depended on this versatile and nutritious food, and without it the country faced starvation. The British held the key to prevent a disaster, but the government's stubbornness and ignorance only made it worse.

The famine was a watershed in Irish history. Relations between Britain and Ireland were deeply and lastingly affected, while Irish emigrants brought about great changes overseas. As thousands of ships left Ireland laden with the desperate poor, little did they suspect that their descendents would reverse centuries of oppression to become among the world's most prosperous and powerful people.

2

# Disaster Awaits

**I**N THE early nineteenth century, Ireland was probably Europe's poorest country. Hundreds of years of subjugation, oppression and discrimination at the hands of the English, its rich and powerful neighbours, had left a long legacy of poverty and misery. In a series of crushed rebellions, lost wars and large-scale confiscations, the natural development of Irish society had been stunted.

In 1690, following the defeat at the Battle of the Boyne of Catholic James II by Protestant William III, the new King of England, a set of Penal Laws were passed. The English Protestants denied the Irish Catholics the right to vote, enter into legal, official or commercial activity, purchase land or get an education. The laws did not succeed in converting the Irish, but the damage they caused was undeniable.

Old estates were wrenched from their owners, family seats were lost forever, and many

Irish nobles fled to sympathetic Catholic countries. By the early eighteenth century, the Catholics, who accounted for three-quarters of the population, owned only 14 per cent of the land. The Irish had effectively become tenants in their own country. In 1801, on the promise of Catholic equality and freedom, Ireland and Britain merged into one nation. It was not until 1829, however, that the Penal Laws were fully repealed.

By this time, Ireland's condition was shocking observers from around the world. The Frenchman, Gustave de Beaumont, lamented: "Misery, naked and famishing, that misery which is vagrant, idle and mendicant, covers the entire country . . . it follows you everywhere and besieges you incessantly . . . it importunes and terrifies you."

Well over half of the rural Irish were living in mud cabins of a single room, without a window for light or a chimney for a peat fire. Only a few could afford furniture; in 1837 the 9,000 inhabitants of Tullahobagly, County Donegal, had only one cart, ten beds and ninety-three chairs between them. The poor shared their little space with their animals, manure piled all about.

For the most part, this unending wretchedness could be put down to the system of land tenure in operation. Unlike England, there was rarely a sense of loyalty and mutual respect between landlord and tenant; instead, the relationship was often tense and hostile, as would be expected between conqueror and vanquished. Many landlords chose to stay away from the troubled country altogether, letting their land for long periods to heartless "middlemen", who were then free to sub-let. These agents were often ruthless and brutal people, out to make as much money as they could through charging exorbitant rents.

Life was extremely hard for the majority who did not own land or could not afford to hire several acres. The landless poor who traded their labour for small plots of land were known as "cottiers". Usually the land was already rented by a tenant farmer and sub-let to them. They would work for the farmer in return for ground to grow their potatoes and a mud cabin. These could be hastily "thrown up" by friends and neighbours, who sometimes made a party of the work, bringing a fiddle and homemade liquor called poteen. Because it was so easy to get a scrap of land without any outlay, and cabins could be erected in little time at no cost and heated by a plentiful turf fire, early marriage and large families were encouraged. The population skyrocketed, and by 1841 there were over eight million people in Ireland, an incredible increase of 172 per cent since 1779. In fact, Ireland had become the most densely populated country in Europe.

Many families allowed their children and children's children to stay with them, rather than turn them out. Without a home, there was little that could be done, as there were no opportunities for employment in Ireland. The once flourishing linen industry of the north-east was well into decline, and families without land and home had no prospects but starvation. They would inhabit roadside ditches or find scant shelter under a few tree roots until death caught

*Children taking peat to school to pay their fees.*

up with them. To avoid this terrible fate, many families had no choice but to keep their future generations with them. Increasing numbers had to eke out a living from diminishing portions of land. Often several families used a tiny scrap of soil only fit to support one family.

The other option was the "conacre", a small plot of land, usually only a quarter of an acre in size, let for a year to a labourer to grow potatoes to feed himself and his family. The labourers could rarely pay the rent at the outset, so they would pay at the end of the year at harvest-time with a share of the produce. If the crop failed, the owner would not get his rent. At the same time, as soon as rent was owing (which it invariably was for these people), the owner could evict them without notice. Having no security, the "conacre" holders lived with the perpetual fear of eviction hanging over them.

In such a system it made good business for the

*(Overleaf) A family leaves their one-roomed cottage in Cork to join relatives who had settled in America in 1832.*

landlords to subdivide property into smaller and smaller plots. Moreover, rents were extortionate – many times more than what was originally paid for the plots – and with growing numbers of people the acute shortage of land only pushed them up further. While extremely profitable for the owners, the "conacre" holders had no chance of breaking out of the system even if the crop was abundant. Whether they were "cottier" or "conacre" holders, the poor ended up paying the most, and the better-off did very well in rents or cheap labour. The whole structure was symptomatic of a country with huge divides between rich and poor, a structure that denied any kind of change or any movement between the two groups.

The entire tottering mass of this system could only be propped up by the potato. No other food could be produced in such large quantities on such pitiful fragments of land. No other food could be cultivated in the wet and acid soils of the west coast, the mountains and the bogs, with just spades for tools. And no other food was so nutritious, both to humans and farm animals.

The humble spud supplies everything the body needs except fats and vitamin A — deficiencies that were remedied in most Irish families with a little buttermilk. An Irish labourer ate a colossal 14 pounds (6.5 kg) of potatoes daily, and together with his family, they consumed 5 tons a year. If an acre of land could yield around 12 tons, on half an acre they had enough to feed themselves, their pigs, chickens, perhaps even a cow. This would be impossible with grain; it would demand six times the acreage and far harder work to produce an equivalent amount.

But the potato was as perilous a crop as it was miraculous. It could not be stored for long periods, and the summer months just before the year's harvest were a time of great hardship. Potatoes from the previous crop would have long been eaten, and the two and a half million labourers had to scrape by as best they could, maybe buying meal on credit at outrageous prices from a local dealer.

Worse still, if the crop failed, there was nothing to eat. There was no other cheap food, and even if limitless credit was available, there was not nearly enough meal to feed millions of starving mouths.

Despite the squalor, the precarious existence, the discrimination, the crushing poverty and privation, the Irish poor were irrepressibly happy people. They were famous for their love of song and dance, their delight in storytelling and conversation, and their hospitality, even when all they had to offer was a bowl of potatoes and a sup of buttermilk. They were fit and strong, on average taller than their English counterparts, and travellers were struck by their beauty. Muddling along from year to year, enjoying their lives where and whenever they could, they squeezed just enough out of their meagre resources to survive.

By the 1840s, overpopulation and terrible poverty made disaster ever more likely. Above all, Ireland's dependence on the potato made the situation critical. Everything rested on the success of the crop. And unknown to the Irish, in 1844 in faraway America, the potatoes had been smitten by a terrible disease.

# BLIGHT

**W**EEKS before the 1845 harvest, it seemed that the Irish potato crop would be exceptionally large. Magazines and papers widely reported predictions of a bumper yield. Meanwhile, a disease had started to appear on the potato crop in the Isle of Wight. No one had seen anything like it before. It spread with alarming pace; throughout August, it tore through England, Holland and France. By September it had reached Ireland. Nevertheless, the plants looked healthy and it seemed that the country had been spared.

In October, however, when it came for the potatoes to be dug up, news of a disaster flooded across the land. An awful blight was rotting the crop. Appearing at first to be sound, the potatoes had quickly developed black bruises inside. Before long, entire crops were decaying into an oozing, black, stinking mush. People were soon in severe distress. The poorest areas in the south and west were the worst hit. Here they depended on the inferior "lumper" potato, a late-maturer, which cruelly had shown no signs of blight until harvest and the weeks after.

To assess the scale of the problem, the government in London sent in a Scientific Commission. At that time there was still limited knowledge of such diseases, and they wrongly diagnosed the cause as a kind of wet-rot created by the damp summer. Their attempts to cure it proved fruitless, nor could they offer a sensible means of salvaging the crop.

In fact, the blight was caused by a fungus, now called *Phytophthora infestans*, which thrives in moist conditions but is not caused by them. It can rapidly affect large areas of land by means of microscopic spores borne on wind and water. If it attacks early in the season, the leaves and stem wither away and the tubers below never develop. If it spreads later in the season, the spores can still penetrate the soil and consume the potato. The popular "lumper" potato was particularly vulnerable to the latter. Unfortunately, it was not until forty years later that a remedy was found.

The Scientific Commission reckoned that half the crop had been destroyed and urgent action was called for to feed the millions who relied on potatoes. Sir Robert Peel, the Tory Prime Minister, saw only one solution – that they be fed on grain. To do this, grain would have to be imported in bulk into the country without restriction. But the idea was impeded by the Corn Laws, a device used to keep prices high and prevent the market from being flooded with cheap imports. Even worse, repeal of the Corn Laws was the hottest political issue of the time, and a large body of farmers and landlords consistently prevented its removal. Peel himself failed to get rid of the laws, and he almost lost his premiership for his efforts. Meanwhile, Ireland's hungry were still without food.

In a stroke of far-sightedness, however, Peel had already secretly ordered £100,000 of Indian corn, or maize, from American suppliers. It was nowhere near enough to feed Ireland, but that was not his intention. His plan was far more cunning: to ensure that the price of grain stayed low. Every time the price looked as though it would leap upwards he ordered his depots to sell grain cheap. The fear of being undercut kept many dealers in Ireland from putting up their prices, and local relief committees were able to buy grain for the country's poor.

Early in 1846, the government also set up around 650 local relief committees and put them under the charge of the relevant landowners and gentry. They received state donations only equal to the charity they could raise and were then expected to provide the local poor with food. In the poorest, most isolated areas in the west and south, the government knew that this would not amount to much and set up outlets to supply food only to those in extreme need. The main problem with the system was the reliance on the landowners' goodwill and public spirit, which was non-existent in many cases.

In addition, public works were started, organized by the Board of Works, to offer employment and wages to the worst-off. Overseeing these works, the relief committees and all relief spending was Sir Charles Trevelyan, the most senior civil servant at the Treasury. An extremely hard-working and able man, he was also strongly in favour of the free market and held a dogged determination that he was always right. He opposed Peel's successful interventionist tactics. Over the coming years, he was to have increasing control of Famine policy. He believed, without compromise, that the Irish should learn to depend on themselves and the resources of their country "instead of having recourse to the assistance of the government on every occasion".

For now at least, Peel had steered Ireland clear of widespread starvation. Surprisingly, pigs had been the main casualties. Without enough to feed them, the poor sold all their animals for grain. It had been necessary, but now they had no safety net if there was a problem in the coming year. The people were also encouraged as much as possible to plant grain instead of potatoes, but it was still not a realistic alternative. Potato seed had been hoarded and was now sown everywhere. The Irish gambled everything on the 1846 harvest being a good one.

# famine

THE summer of 1846 looked promising for Ireland. The potato crop seemed plentiful and a new Whig government, led by Lord John Russell, came into power promising to repeal the Corn Laws. But in the course of a week everything had changed. The weather had been warm and wet and the blight reappeared everywhere. This letter to Trevelyan from an Irish priest was one of the first signs of the impending catastrophe: "On the 27th of last month I passed from Cork to Dublin and this doomed plant bloomed in all the luxuriance of an abundant harvest. Returning on the 3rd instant, I beheld, with sorrow, one wide waste of putrefying vegetation. In many places the wretched people were seated on the fences of their decaying gardens, wringing their hands and wailing bitterly the destruction that had left them foodless".

Nine-tenths of the crop had been destroyed

and four million people were without food for the second year running. They were exhausted. They had struggled through a difficult year and the lean summer months. They had used up every resource in the process. Now they had nothing and stared death in the face. The situation demanded swift and efficient handling from the British administration.

Trevelyan and the Whigs, however, were more concerned with the play of market forces and ending Ireland's "cancer of dependency". They wanted "Irish property to support Irish poverty" by making the Irish landowners shoulder the burden. They concentrated relief in the public works, which were to be funded by local landlords.

Hundreds of thousands of starving people came seeking work. The Board of Works was completely overwhelmed and had no idea how to employ so many people. They were set to pointless tasks, digging up and remaking perfectly good roads or just cracking stones for the sake of work. Meanwhile, food prices soared

*Artist's portrayal of a grim scene in the west of Ireland. A girl dying of starvation and fever is shown in a typical mean interior.*

and the labourers' meagre wages were far from enough to support their families. Starving masses combed the fields, bogs and shores, searching for nettles, roots, seaweed and even rotting potatoes (that made them weaker still), anything at all to assuage the great hunger.

*Women gathering seaweed on the coast of Clare.*

To compound the misery, the winter of 1846–7 was the worst in living memory. The Board decided the weather was so severe that the labourers should get half wages and not come to work, but the poor would not let their income fall any further. Riots broke out, and where they did the government ordered the works to close. One British works manager described the effects of this mass punishment: "although a man not easily moved, I confess myself unmanned by the extent and intensity of the suffering I witnessed, more especially amongst the women and little children, crowds of whom were to be seen scattered over the turnip fields, like a flock of famishing crows, devouring the raw turnips. Mothers half-naked, shivering in the snow and sleet, uttering exclamations of despair whilst their children were screaming with hunger; I am a match for anything else I may meet with here, but this I cannot stand".

By the beginning of 1847, local relief committees were collapsing and people were dying. Again, the remote regions suffered the worst. Skibbereen in County Cork on the south coast was typical. It was brought to the world's attention by a series of sketches made for a newspaper. The artist said: "In Skibbereen I saw the dying, the living and the dead, lying indiscriminately upon the same floor, without anything between them and the cold earth, save a few miserable rags upon them". Dogs devoured the unburied corpses.

The public was shocked and charity money poured in. Queen Victoria herself donated £2,000. The Quakers organized soup kitchens

*A corpse being taken away in Skibbereen.*

and distributed turnip and parsnip seed for the coming year. Large amounts of food and money poured in from all over America, including one contribution from the Choctaw Indians. The United States was waging war with Mexico at the time, but still managed to spare two warships, the *Jamestown* and the *Macedonian*, to ferry supplies to Ireland. Even the British government changed direction. Impressed by the Quakers, it set up a network of soup kitchens, and although the remotest places, like Skibbereen, did not have one until the summer, they were far more effective in saving lives, not to mention far cheaper, than the public works.

But in 1847, starvation was not the biggest killer. Malnutrition had left millions of people vulnerable to disease. As the destitute swarmed towards the towns or centres of work and relief, conditions were ripe for an epidemic. Typhus swept through the population, passed on by lice,

*(Overleaf) The* USS Jamestown *which was loaned by Congress to carry relief supplies to Cork in 1847.*

and killed doctors, priests and aid workers along with the poor. Dysentery, known as "bloody flux", and wasting diseases, caused by terrible malnutrition, such as marasmus and "famine dropsy" (oedema) also killed thousands. Burials, where they occurred, were quick and without ceremony, bodies flung into makeshift graves by the side of roads. In many cases there were no records, but where they existed it became clear that a great number of people had perished. In just one week in April, 2,613 inmates of the workhouses alone had died. The death toll was running into hundreds of thousands.

The massive social collapse sent panic through the country. Families sold everything they could to raise enough money to leave the country. Floods of desperate people surged to the ports, abandoning everything they had, to start a new life abroad. But for those who could not or would not flee, the situation only deteriorated further.

*Paying for passage. The emigration agent's office, Cork (from the Illustrated London News 1851).*

# eviction

THE fact that the potato crop did not fail in the summer of 1847 was another cruel twist of fate for Ireland. The harvest may have been good, but the famine was far from over. There had been a shortage of seed and a lack of money to buy it. The people had spent all their energies earning pennies at the public works; they had neither the time nor the strength to plough and tend to their plots. The harvest had been excellent, but only a fraction of the land had been cultivated. And since the closure of the works, no one had money to buy the food that had been produced. In short, famine conditions were in full swing.

The British, however, ignored all that and pretended that the troubles were over. Trevelyan, still in charge of relief, decided to go on holiday to France. Their management of Ireland took a definite turn for the worse. They ordered the closure of the public works. And they did not intervene with exports, so much Irish-produced food was taken from where it was most needed and shipped to England. Three million people were now being fed everyday by the soup kitchens, but to emphasize that they were just a temporary measure, the government began to phase them out too. With a financial crisis emerging in Britain, they no longer thought that saving Irish lives was worth their precious money.

In June the government passed the Poor Law Extension Act, which sought to change the social organization of Ireland by removing inefficient and penniless landlords and transforming the peasantry into waged labourers on productive large-scale farms. It forced able-bodied people to give up all their means of support before they were allowed to enter the workhouse for food.

Workhouses were widely hated for their brutal regimes, back-breaking work and segregation by age and sex. Many poor families with a little land were faced with a fearful choice: either leave their homes for the inescapable misery of the workhouse, or stay and risk starvation. To fund the

*Eviction scene from the* Illustrated London News, *1848*

workhouses and relief, the Act made landlords pay rates for themselves and for tenants with holdings worth under £4. The government knew that, to avoid this extra cost, the landlords would evict their poorer tenants, so ridding Ireland of thousands of its tiny, inefficient plots.

By October 1847, the soup kitchens were all

closed but the people were still in desperate need. The new Act started to take effect. Landlords, faced with rates they could never hope to pay and with thousands of hungry mouths to feed, made the brutal decision to evict. It was not a hard task to find tenants who had not paid their rent following two years of calamity. In fact, in the poorest regions of the west, in the most neglected estates of Clare, Galway and Mayo, the people had lived on tiny scraps of soil without paying rent or having interference from landlords for years. Eviction notices were served to the poor throughout the country.

Very soon hundreds of thousands of destitute people – their little cabins and cottages "tumbled" in minutes by landlords' agents who pulled down the turf roofs and kicked in the walls – thronged Ireland's wintry roads. Where they resisted, the British army helped remove them, and once they were out of their homes they were forbidden to return and their neighbours were forbidden to shelter them. In some places, entire villages were evicted in a day and homeless families were sent without food or hope into a starving, broken country. They found refuge where they could, making *scalps* or *scalpeens* by digging holes in bogs and covering them with turf. But often they were pried from these too. To most, eviction meant death and, indeed, huge numbers perished.

Others chose the workhouse, some only because they knew they would be buried in a coffin when they died inside its walls. And die they did, since the workhouses were now filled to bursting. Kilrush workhouse, for example, built for 800, had now stuffed 5,000 paupers within. Conditions were pitiful. Tired, malnourished people were jammed into filthy, cramped quarters. Disease gripped the workhouses. In Kilrush, the pig slaughterhouse was converted into a fever hospital, but its name hung heavy over it. In one week, all but two of its 101 patients died there.

In 1848, blight ravaged the potato crop yet again, and towards the end of the year the funds of the charities were running out. The Irish had

long lost the sympathy of the British public, who believed that the country had somehow brought the problem on itself. Such was God's punishment for the "feckless" Catholics, they thought. The Quakers, who had done so much good, finally gave up, complaining that "the government alone could raise the funds and carry out the measures necessary in many districts to save the lives of the people".

The early months of 1849 were perhaps the worst of any in the course of the Famine. Now in its fourth year, the people "were skinned to the bone" by its cumulative ruin. British officials working in Ireland sent repeated pleas for aid and relief, but in vain. Edward Twisleton, the chief commissioner of the poor law officials there, resigned in March 1849 saying that "the destitution here is so horrible, and the indifference of the House of Commons to it so manifest, that [I am] an unfit agent of a policy that must be one of extermination".

Still the British government stood by its non-interventionist policies, preferring to let events follow their "natural course". Trevelyan stuck obstinately to his *laissez faire* (or "leave alone") obsessions and rejected action, claiming "what the patient now requires is rest and quiet and time for the remedies which have been given to operate".

In these final years of the famine, the government spent almost nothing on Ireland. The cost in human suffering, however, was incalculable. The population had dwindled by two and half million and well over a million of those had died. The poor, the very young and the elderly perished in the greatest numbers, and countless doctors and relief workers went with them. The government's response to the crisis, especially after the autumn of 1847, had been appalling. Twisleton had said that a "comparatively trifling sum" was needed for Britain "to spare itself the deep disgrace of permitting any of [its] miserable fellow subjects to die of starvation". But the economic beliefs of the time had overshadowed all sense of compassion and humanity, leading to a tragedy until then unheard of in Europe.

# emigration

FACED with eviction, disease, starvation and death, hundreds of thousands of Irish fled their country. Emigration began many years before the Famine, but after the horrors of 1846, the next decade saw an exodus of almost two million people, a quarter of the population.

The country of choice was the United States, land of hope and opportunity, long since free from its British colonial masters. Canada, known then as British North America, was, however, much cheaper. The timber ships had previously sailed back to Canada without a cargo, but now their owners saw a fantastic chance to make money carrying human ballast. All sorts of unseaworthy ships, coasters and colliers, entirely unsuitable for crossing the Atlantic, were

*(Opposite) In good weather, thirty people at a time were allowed on deck to exercise.*

readied in the rush to cash in. The worst of these were called "coffin ships".

By law the ships were supposed to provide their passengers adequate food, water and space. But once the fare had been paid, the owners had no cares for passenger comfort, and such was the state of Ireland at the time there was no one to enforce the law. Emigrants, many already diseased and malnourished, were crammed into the lightless holds beneath the deck and given "berths". Makeshift bunks had been slapped on to the ships' beams, in two or more rows if the ship was large enough. For their "berths", adults were allotted a quarter of a bunk, and children an eighth, just nine inches of space.

At sea, provisions were distributed daily, but the food was often rotting and the water contaminated. Not surprisingly, outbreaks of dysentery were common. Sailors went to the toilet over the sea, clinging to a tiny rail on the ship's bows, but passengers were often too scared, frail or embarrassed to follow suit. They went, if there was space, to the cable tiers beneath them. When the hatch of the hold was bolted down in severe weather, with people suffering from dysentery all about and four or more stuffed to a bunk, the smell and conditions must have been unimaginable. All this, day after day, on a journey that could take three months.

Nothing on these ships was more disastrous, however, than typhus. The cramped, unsanitary quarters, the impossibility of washing clothes and bedding (if they had any), gave the lice that carried the disease free reign. Medical examinations before boarding were cursory at best, and it only took one infected person to bring down most of the ship.

It was a terrifying and little-understood disease; no one knew how it was spread or how to cure it. First the body took on a darkened hue, hence the name "black fever", the victim's temperature shot up and their limbs twitched and flailed uncontrollably. Sores developed into gangrene, sometimes at the loss of fingers and toes,

*(Overleaf) Below decks on a famine ship.*

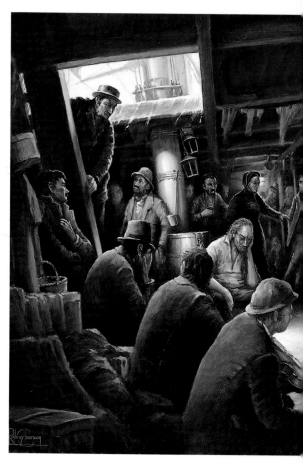

44

producing "an almost intolerable stench". One doctor remarked that when the odour was in the air he was "always seized with most violent retching" and was "forcibly driven back by the smell". Of course, on a ship there was no escaping it.

The voyage itself was fraught with danger too, with violent storms and towering waves capsizing helpless ships. One ship, having just set sail from Westport, County Mayo, went down with all on board to the horror of friends and relatives who were still waving goodbye. The *Hannah,* a small Irish-owned ship, also sank. On its way to Quebec it hit an iceberg at four in the morning. The cowardly captain jumped ship with his senior officers as soon as he realized it was going down, leaving the passengers and the rest of the crew to their fate. The ship took forty minutes before it went under, giving them enough time to scramble on to the ice. In the struggle to get off, fifty or sixty fell between the boat and the iceberg and were crushed between them. The 129 survivors waited for 15 hours in their thin night-clothes, hugging each other for warmth,

*The* Hannah, *which hit an iceberg*

before the *Nicaragua* emerged from the gloom and saved them. The captain of the *Hannah* was disgraced when he landed at Quebec.

These were the risks the emigrants were prepared to take to reach America and escape the terrible famine. When they made their destination, however, their troubles were not at an end. Any ships that had sick passengers had to stop at quarantine stations. Everyone, whether ill or not, had to land at the station and was kept in isolation until the ship was cleared to leave. Their first taste of the new life and the New World was indeed a bitter one, as they were forced into quarantine. Grosse Ile, an island thirty miles downstream from Quebec, was the station for the new arrivals to Canada. For half the year it was locked in ice, and during the thaw of May 1847 the officials braced themselves for Ireland's starving.

The *Syria* was the first ship to arrive. Of its 241 passengers, nine had died on board and 84 had fever. The hospital had beds for 150, over half of which had been taken after only one ship. Dr Douglas, the station's chief medic, sensed catastrophe and urgently asked for help from his government. They sent him £135 to erect a new hospital shed, but Douglas had learned that over ten thousand emigrants were already on their way. By the end of May, 36 ships had docked with a total of 13,000 emigrants on board. The suffering had been unbearable: the *Avon* had lost nearly half of its 552 passengers, while of 476 on the *Virginius*, 158 had died at sea and a further 106 had fever.

In July, there were 2,500 sick, strewn about the island in every available outhouse and building. Conditions were dreadful. The station's few doctors soon became ill and died, and at one point Douglas was working alone for the thousands in his charge. Nurses were impossible to hire and no one volunteered. The fear and repulsion that the Irish understandably felt for the fever led Douglas to remark that "the nearest relatives abandon each other whenever they can". The only few who offered to help turned out to be robbing the dead and dying.

And still more "spectre-like wretches", "emaciated", "cadaverous", "feeble" passengers stumbled from the ships. In August, the Anglican Bishop of Montreal saw some new arrivals lying by the church screaming for water. In the tents he found others sleeping in the mud; it was raining and they had no bedding. In another was a dying child covered in vermin.

The quarantine process had to be accelerated and Douglas allowed the "healthy" to go on to Quebec and Montreal. As numbers increased at Grosse Ile, an "avalanche of diseased and dying people [was] thrown daily" on the wharfs in the heart of Montreal, its most populated district. Epidemics soon raged in Canada's cities, killing nearly fifteen thousand people.

It is impossible to say exactly how many died during the years of emigration. In 1847 alone, over 100,000 Irish left for Canada, the majority of those quarantined at Grosse Ile. Thousands died in the crossing, and many thousands more were thrown into the mass graves at the quarantine stations. It is thought as many as 40,000 people lost their lives that year in their search for a new beginning.

# the united states

OR most the goal was to get to the
United States and out of the hands of the
British. In 1847 the bedraggled survivors
of Grosse Ile made their way to the border. The
Americans tried to stem the flow, but the
numbers were overwhelming. Boston was
swamped with over 37,000 immigrants,
swelling its population by a third. Some 53,000
made for New York, bringing typhus with them.

Swindlers, known as "runners" or "man-
catchers", and usually Irish too, greeted them in
these cities. The confusion of the whole
experience for the new arrivals made it easy work
for the crooks to steal their baggage, or lead them
to ruthless landlords who took all their money
through extortionate rents. Some had come so far,
and been through so much, only to have all their
possessions tricked from them at the last hurdle.

Many, utterly penniless, drifted towards the
slums. Others ended up in the prisons and

lunatic asylums, but the majority found work in the worst-paid, most-dangerous jobs. The United States was deeply anti-Catholic at that time, and prejudice was widespread. "No Irish need apply" was the recurring slogan that excluded them from most employment.

Only the richer could afford passage to America, as the US officials had introduced a bond system making ship-owners responsible for their passengers, thus forcing ticket prices up. When the situation in Ireland only worsened in 1848, many of its wealthier inhabitants decided it was time to leave too. Even for them the voyage was a terrible ordeal, and during the Famine years, out of almost 3,000 crossings, only 325 ships made the journey more than once. Conditions at the quarantine stations, though, were generally much better than they had been in Canada.

The talents and skills of this later wave doubtless dampened some of the hostility towards the Irish. Gradually the Irish community heaved itself out of the ghettos. Advance was painfully slow, but many eventually found work as unskilled labourers. In the pioneering years of the United States, the Irish were the workers behind the great roads and railways; they manned the factories and dug in the mines.

Other groups were reluctant to give up the rural life. One was led by Father Thomas Hore from Wexford, who wanted to help his congregation escape the misery and squalor of Ireland. His vision of being free, owning land, with "no rent, tithe or tax to pay", being able to worship God "without incurring the ill-will of his brother man" persuaded over a thousand of his parishioners to start afresh in America. They sailed south to New Orleans and took a steamer up the Mississippi and Arkansas rivers, deep into the American heartland. From Little Rock they trekked a thousand miles further north, to Iowa, where the lush meadows and woodlands reminded them of home. Here they settled, and with their

*(Overleaf) Father Hore's passengers from the* Ticonderoga *queue on the quay at New Orleans to join a paddle steamer to take them up the Mississippi to Wexford, Iowa.*

collected savings bought 2,157 acres of farmland. They built houses, farms and a church, and at last they could enjoy a free and prosperous life in their new home, which they called Wexford.

Slowly the Irish communities in America grew in strength. Centuries of resistance to persecution in their homeland had made them adept at organizing themselves into "combinations" and secret societies. As trade unionism blossomed in the United States, the Irish-Americans became an increasingly prominent and commanding force.

Many Irish still had the horrors of the Famine years fresh in their minds; their image of Ireland was one frozen in time. With the distance of a few thousand miles, they saw more clearly how badly the British government had let them down. In 1848, a radical group called the "Young Irelanders" had led a woefully ill-prepared rebellion against the British in Ballingarry, County Tipperary. It ended in an almost farcical scuffle in "Widow McCormack's cabbage patch", and the leaders were quickly rounded up and transported to Tasmania. Several of them soon escaped and, like

*Many hopeful emigrants found passage on* Erin Go Bragh, *which means "Ireland Forever". She sailed out of Liverpool for New York.*

millions of others, headed for America. The anti-British sentiment there was fierce, and with the "Young Irelanders" to articulate it, a sense of bitter grievance and nationalism intensified.

The Catholic Church grew in wealth and respectability and provided education and community to the Irish-Americans. Over the years, national pride, community action and the Church propelled them up the social ladder, and by 1900 only 15 per cent were still unskilled labourers. Sixty years later, they had amongst the highest average incomes in America.

The ultimate mark of their success was the election in 1960 of the first Catholic Irish-American president, John F. Kennedy. His great-grandfather had emigrated to Boston from New Ross, County Wexford, in 1847. President Kennedy symbolized how much the Irish could achieve when the burden of British oppression had been lifted from them. Once the persecuted masses of the poorest country in Europe, the Irish had become the leaders of the most powerful nation on Earth.